The LEAKEYS

The Family That Traced Human Origins to Africa

The LEAKEYS

The Family That Traced Human Origins to Africa

ROSEN
PUBLISHING

Angie Timmons

Published in 2021 by The Rosen Publishing Group, Inc.
29 East 21st Street, New York, NY 10010

Library of Congress Cataloging-in-Publication Data

Names: Timmons, Angie.
Title: The Leakeys: the family that traced human origins to Africa / Angie Timmons.
Description: New York : Rosen Publishing, 2021. | Series: Scientific collaboration | Includes glossary and index.
Identifiers: ISBN 9781725342408 (pbk.) | ISBN 9781725342415 (library bound)
Subjects: LCSH: Leakey, L. S. B. (Louis Seymour Bazett), 1903-1972--Juvenile literature. | Leakey, Mary D. (Mary Douglas), 1913-1996--Juvenile literature. | Leakey, L. S. B. (Louis Seymour Bazett), 1903-1972. | Leakey, Mary D. (Mary Douglas), 1913-1996. | Anthropologists--Kenya--Biography--Juvenile literature. | Fossil hominids--Africa, East--Juvenile literature.
Classification: LCC GN21.L37 T56 2021 | DDC 301.092 B--dc23

Printed in China

Photo Credits: Cover, pp. 3, 53 Melville B. Grosvenor/National Geographic Image Collection/Getty Images; cover, p. 3 (right) Bettmann/Getty Images; p. 7 Everett Collection Historical/Alamy Stock Photo; p. 11 Encyclopædia Britannica/Universal Images Group/Getty Images; pp. 12-13 ullstein bild/Getty Images; pp. 14-15 Javier Trueba/MSF/Science Source; pp. 18-19 Robert F. Sisson/National Geographic Image Collection/Getty Images; p. 21 John Reader/Science Source; pp. 22-23 Brian C. Weed/Shutterstock.com; p. 28 © iStockphoto.com/pierivb; p. 31 © iStockphoto.com/JordiStock; p. 33 SeM/Universal Images Group/Getty Images; pp. 35, 38, 58-59 Marion Kaplan/Alamy Stock Photo; p. 37 Dorling Kindersley ltd/Alamy Stock Photo; p. 41 Keystone/Hulton Archive/Getty Images; pp. 42-43 Robert F. Sisson/National Geographic Image Collection/Getty Images; p. 45 Michael Nicholson/Corbis Historical/Getty Images; p. 47 Helen Marcus/Science Source/Getty Images; p. 51 Werner Forman/Universal Images Group/Getty Images; p. 54 © AP Images; p. 60 Danita Delimont/Alamy Stock Photo; p. 62 Gilbert M. Grosvenor/National Geographic Image Collection/Getty Images; p. 65 Hindustan Times/Getty Images; pp. 66-67 Brent Stirton/Getty Images; cover and interior pages graphic elements (background icons) LineByLine/Shutterstock.com, (atom) Mechanic Design/Shutterstock.com

CPSIA Compliance Information: Batch #BSR20. For further information contact Rosen Publishing, New York, New York at 1-800-237-9932.

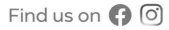
Find us on

CONTENTS

Introduction

One sweltering day in the hills of Western Kenya, four-year-old Richard Leakey was tired, hot, and hungry. He complained to his parents that he wanted to go home for lunch. They were busy digging for fossils while their bored young son waited on them. In response, his father shouted something most young children would never hear from their parents: "Go and find your own bone!"

But Richard Leakey was not like most children his age, and his parents, Louis and Mary Leakey, were definitely not like most other parents: They were famous paleoanthropologists (scientists who study human origins) and archaeologists who had achieved worldwide notoriety for their findings in Africa.

Knowing his dedicated scientific parents would never stop working just because he wanted to go home, Richard took his father's advice and started digging. Upon spotting a small bone, he began to carefully dig it out using the techniques he'd observed his parents use since he was a toddler. The bone got bigger. As he kept digging around it, he saw that the bone had teeth. All of a sudden, his boredom and other complaints were gone. He went quiet, carefully viewing this find. His parents eventually noticed

Mary and Louis Leakey dedicated their lives to their work. Along with their children, they made some of the greatest discoveries of all time.

he'd been missing for a while and went in search of their small son. Within minutes, Richard was pushed aside as Louis and Mary enthusiastically took over the excavation. What Richard had found was the first complete jaw of an extinct species of pig ever discovered. His find resulted in an entirely new excavation project led by his parents.[1]

By the time Richard found the pig jawbone, his father had been digging for fossils in Africa for about two decades. In the 1930s, Louis, who had grown up in Kenya as the son of British missionaries, rocked the scientific community when he found a fossil proving that human life had evolved in Africa, disproving the long-held theory that human life had evolved in Asia. With this find, Louis irrevocably altered the course of scientific thinking and research priorities. When Louis wed Mary Nicol, an English artist and archaeologist, in 1936, the couple made Africa their home and devoted their lives to archaeological finds that consistently challenged scientific perceptions about human origins.

Perhaps as intriguing as Louis and Mary's archaeological finds is that paleoarchaeology became a family business when they had children. The couple famously brought their three sons, Jonathan, Richard, and Philip, to their excavation sites as soon as Mary could return to work after childbirth. The three sons have had varying levels of involvement in their parents' chosen field, with Richard and his wife, Meave, especially making scientific headlines with their findings.

Louis and Mary's legacy has been carried on by their descendants, making the family—both then and now—a truly shining example of the extraordinary achievements made possible through collaboration. Over nearly one hundred years, the Leakeys have continued to contribute to the family business, making them the First Family of Paleontology.

CHAPTER ONE

Origins

In an 1871 publication called *The Descent of Man*, the English scientist Charles Darwin (1809–1882) predicted that human origins would be found in Africa. His prediction was based on some evolutionary human traits, such as walking on two feet and the use of tools.[1] However, neither Darwin nor his peers had much evidence to either support or deny his theory.

Darwin wasn't the first to look for a link between modern humans and ancient ancestors. A few scientists had sought evidence of human evolution and hominids, a family of primates that includes both extinct and existing species. Their theories revolved around the evolution of the species *Homo sapiens* (modern humans) and the more encompassing genus *Homo*, which includes *Homo sapiens* and some closely related extinct species. *Homo* had been the subject of debate among scientists who predated Darwin and his 1859 book *On the Origin of Species*, which is considered the foundation of evolutionary biology.[2] These scientists theorized that great apes were closely related to humans, but only after

Darwin's work did scientists begin considering that humans had evolved from other species rather than merely sharing characteristics. What all these late nineteenth-century scientists lacked was the "missing link"—or fossil evidence to prove humans had evolved from other species.[3]

"Out of Asia"

Frustrated by lack of evidence to link modern humans to earlier species, Dutch anatomist Eugène Dubois traveled to present-day Indonesia in the late 1880s to look for evidence. He chose this area based on contemporary theories that humans were closely related to certain apes that lived in the region, leading him to believe he was traveling to the cradle of civilization. By the early 1890s, Dubois had found many fossils, including some he believed belonged to one ancient individual. The characteristics of the fossils, including bones indicating the individual had walked upright, led Dubois to claim he'd found the missing link between modern humans and their evolutionary predecessors. The collected body parts, which were estimated to be between seven hundred thousand and one million years old, were called Java Man due to where they were found: the Indonesian island of Java.[4] Thus, the "Out of Asia" theory began, with scientists flocking to Asia to search for—and often find—other fossils from the same general time period in which Java Man would have lived. Most of these fossils were certainly from the genus *Homo*, and some were even from the species *Homo erectus*, or "upright walkers," who displayed bipedalism. The "Out of Asia" theory of human evolution prevailed throughout the late nineteenth century and through much of the first half of the twentieth century. In the 1930s, Louis Leakey would challenge the prevailing "Out of Asia" theory.

Early scientific theories about evolution centered around the fossils of upright species that lived approximately 1,700,000 to 200,000 years ago in Asia.

12 inches

40 cm

Personal Origins

By the time he started digging for fossils in Africa in the 1920s, Louis Leakey already had a strong link to the continent. He was born in Kenya in 1903 to British missionary parents. At the time, Kenya was known as British East Africa and was controlled by the British. When Britain became heavily embroiled in World War I (1914–1918), the Leakey family elected to stay in Kenya. Young Louis grew up close to the native Kikuyu, the largest ethnic group in Kenya. As a boy, he traded British cultural traditions with their Kikuyu traditions. The Kikuyu taught Louis to hunt and exist in the Kenyan wilderness. He even learned their language, was initiated into their tribe, and eventually moved into his own Kikuyu-style hut on his parents' property. Through his adventures with the Kikuyu, Louis developed an appreciation for anthropology and began collecting things he found in nature, including prehistoric stone tools he discovered in riverbeds—his earliest archaeological finds.[5]

As a child, Louis Leakey befriended members of Kenya's Kikuyu tribe. Young Louis and his Kikuyu friends traded cultural traditions, inspiring Louis to pursue anthropology.

Divided Origins

Though he had a divided identity due to his family's British citizenship and his childhood in Kenya, Louis thought of Kenya as home. This would become evident when Louis was sixteen and the Leakey family was finally able to return to England after World War I. He enrolled first at a private boys' secondary school and then Cambridge University. He had trouble fitting in due to the characteristics he'd picked up as a close companion of the Kikuyu (including how he talked and even how he walked), which his English classmates found foreign and strange. In Kenya, Louis had been taught by a tutor and spent his free time wandering the Kenyan wilderness. He struggled against his English schools' restrictions and strict schedules. Still, he managed to make a name for himself at Cambridge, where he studied anthropology and archaeology.

The Leakey Origin Quest Begins

In the mid-1920s, Louis worked on a fossil-finding expedition in what's now Tanzania while healing from a sports injury he suffered at Cambridge. This w first real glimpse into the fields he'd been studying a He began to seriously question human origins. After hi Louis returned to college in England, graduating in 19 doctorate in African prehistory. Although the prevailing the time was the "Out of Asia" theory, Louis Leakey ag Darwin's theory that humans originated out of Africa this time, very early human remains had been d in South Africa, but Louis was determined to return t

In 1924, the Taung Child fossil (*left*) was found in South Africa. It belonged to a bipedal ape that lived three to two million years ago and shared similarities with the modern chimpanzee (*right*).

stomping grounds in eastern Africa and find more compelling evidence of early human origins. He ignored a Cambridge professor's suggestion that he begin excavations in Asia, secured money from investors, and by January 1927, Louis set up his first excavation camp in Kenya. He lived in a mud hut. Natives helped

Gamble's Cave

A farmer who lived near Louis's first excavation site told Louis about a cave on his property that might yield interesting results. The farmer was right. Louis and his team dug 14 feet (4.3 meters) underground in the cave and found artifacts, including stone tools and pottery, and fossils and bone fragments. They dug through three more layers of rock, finding more artifacts and fossils. At the fourth level, they found objects that were more than twenty thousand years old. Louis felt vindicated that he'd found evidence of prehistoric people in Africa.[6]

him dig for fossils. Louis and his team found some skeletons, tools, and pottery.[7]

A Forgotten Origin Story

While Louis dug around Kenya in 1927, he met a young Englishwoman, Wilfrida ("Frida") Avern, who visited his excavation site out of curiosity. Louis quickly fell for Frida and asked her to marry him. She said she'd think about it. In late 1927, Louis hauled one hundred crates full of his Kenyan findings to England. He shared his findings with other scientists and with anthropology students he taught to earn some extra money.

When Louis returned to Kenya in 1928, he came with a companion: his new wife, Frida.[8] Over the next few years, Louis and Frida struggled to balance Louis's tireless passion for excavations and Frida's concerns about raising their baby daughter, Priscilla, in what she considered the dangerous wilds of eastern Africa. Frida preferred the comfort and familiarity of England, but Louis's heart would always be in Africa. A month after their son Colin was born in December 1933, Louis and Frida separated.[9] Louis Leakey and the family he had with Mary would one day be the subject of news stories, but the story of Frida, Priscilla, and Colin faded into the background.

While his marriage with Frida fractured and broke, Louis's archaeological appetite grew to form a firm foundation for his future family.

Parallel Paths

When Louis returned to Kenya in 1928, he continued excavating Gamble's Cave. He found two human skeletons. Nearby, his team found hand axes. Based on the area's geology, Louis estimated the axes were between forty and fifty thousand years old. Louis, electrified by his finds, continued to excavate in the Gamble's Cave area. He and his team found bits of bone that, once pieced together, revealed part of a skeleton. The rocks where fossils were found were left in place, plastered, and then hauled to camp by teams of men.[1] The rocks were the evidence Louis desperately needed to legitimize his sometimes over-eager opinions about how old his findings were—evidence he would find at a new dig he started in 1931 at a remote area called Olduvai Gorge in the region now known as Tanzania.

Olduvai Gorge in Tanzania was a geological wonder for Louis Leakey. The gorge's geological layers served as a timeline for the fossils found within.

A Scientific Paradise

Layers of rock form the earth. Each layer was formed at a certain time, or geological era. When fossils and other artifacts are found in a certain layer of rock, they can usually be dated based on that layer's era. Free from modern disruptions such as roads and settlements, Olduvai Gorge's fossils rose in steep layers above the floor of the gorge. Five layers were visible without even digging for them, and they all showed evidence of having formed in distinct geological eras. Louis Leakey reverently called Olduvai "a geological layer cake."[2]

Founding a Reputation

At Olduvai, Louis found fossils ranging from twenty thousand to two million years old. He and his team excavated more hand axes near the skeletal remains of an ancient hippo. They concluded ancient hunters had killed and eaten the animal at that site. He found the bones of a creature that appeared to be akin to an elephant in a location that dated the bones to two million years ago. The team found stone tools in every Olduvai layer. Those from the bottommost layer—the oldest tools that had yet been found in the entire world—were rocks with rudimentary edges used for cutting.[3] As the stone tools got more sophisticated in the upper layers, Louis and his team got a firsthand look at how humans got more sophisticated with time.

As Olduvai's resources depleted, Louis and his team had to decamp. In 1932, he began working nearby in Kanam. In the rain and mud, Louis found more animal bones, some of which were similar to those he'd found at Olduvai. He even found a hominid jaw and teeth, leading him to conclude the hominid had lived

In 1932, Louis Leakey found the Kanam jaw fragment (*lower left*) and fragments of a skull found in Kanjera. Leakey believed they were from the oldest ancestors of modern humans.

21

in the same era as the creatures (about two million years ago). Louis proclaimed these finds the oldest hominid fossils in Africa, perhaps the world.[4]

Though former professors and his family members had cautioned Louis against prematurely pronouncing that his finds were older than anyone else's, he had difficulty reining in his enthusiasm. His race to prove the Kanam jaw was the oldest hominid evidence ever found led him to leave the excavation site in a sorry state. He merely marked the spot where he'd found the jaw with some pegs, took some pictures of the site, and went off to publish articles about the find and bring the jaw to England for scientific review. Only one of the scientists who reviewed the jaw believed it to be older than five hundred thousand years old. Another, Percy Boswell, decided he needed to see the excavation site himself. Three years had passed since Louis had been at Kanam, and in that time, the pegs marking the site had been lost and he couldn't pin down where he'd found the jaw. When Boswell arrived to find this disarray, he was furious. He criticized Louis publicly in an article that was published all around the world.[5] Louis had not only failed to prove his theory that the jaw was the oldest hominid evidence in the world—he'd failed to make a good name for himself in the scientific community. He would pay for his mistakes for years.

A Woman in a Man's World

Mary Nicol was born in London in 1913 to artists Erskine and Cecilia Nicol. Mary's parents liked to travel, so as a young girl, she got to see exciting things such as Egyptian mummies and ancient tools in French museums. She saw prehistoric paintings in caves in France and even dug through the dirt in one of those caves to find rudimentary tools likely used by prehistoric people, such as flint blades. Like her future husband, Louis Leakey, Mary's childhood exposure to these ancient treasures piqued her interest in the people who'd created them. Also like young Louis,

The prehistoric stone circle at Stonehenge in southwest England is about 4,500 years old. The stones' history and the people who erected them inspired Mary Nicol's anthropological interests.

23

Mary grew to like animals, and she overcame her fear of wild ones; when her father got sick with cancer while the Nicols were staying in France, she took long walks on which she saw foxes and wild boars.[6]

When her father died, Mary and her mother returned to London. Again, like her future husband, she struggled in school. She was expelled from one school for refusing to recite a poem in front of her classmates. She was expelled from a second school for causing an explosion in chemistry class. Mary's mother wanted her to pursue art, like her parents. So she did—to a point. She couldn't forget the ancient treasures she'd seen on her childhood trips to other countries, though. She secretly wanted to become an archaeologist. Her respect for the ancient grew when she visited Stonehenge, a mysterious circle of prehistoric rocks in southwestern England. Later, she would recall feeling like an intruder in that ancient space and wondering, "How did these huge stones get here? And who put them in this circle?"[7]

On their way back to London from Stonehenge, Mary and her mother stopped at another ancient stone circle, Avebury, and they learned an archaeological dig was happening nearby. Mary's mother contacted the man in charge of the dig and got permission for Mary to visit the site. There, she met a famous female archaeologist, Dorothy Liddell.

Like most scientific and other professional fields at that time, men dominated the field of archaeology. Mary's chances of becoming an archaeologist seemed slim, especially considering she had no formal education. Meeting Liddell was a significant moment for Mary—she realized a woman could become an archaeologist, and she committed to pursuing that dream. She took relevant classes and went to interesting lectures at museums whenever possible. She joined Liddell on digs in England for three summers. She was even able to merge her family's artistic talents with her personal passion in archaeology when Liddell hired her to draw pictures of items they found on excavations.[8] Her drawings got the attention of another famous female archaeologist, Gertrude Caton-Thompson, who asked Mary to draw some tools she'd found in Egypt. Impressed with Mary's work, Caton-Thompson asked Mary to join her for a big lecture at the Royal Anthropological Institute in London. Mary accepted the invitation. In doing so, she changed the course of history.[9]

CHAPTER THREE

True Love and Tumult

After his Kanam findings, Louis spent a few years in London. His young family was there, but that wasn't the primary reason for Louis's presence in England. He wanted to convince the scientific community that at Kanam, he'd discovered part of the oldest hominid ever found, so he gave lectures about his African excavations and Kanam especially. These lectures were critical for Louis to make a name for himself among the scientific community and to pique the interest of wealthy people who might be willing to fund the work he wanted to continue in Africa. This was often difficult to achieve in the 1930s, a decade plagued with global economic downturn. Louis was left adrift in London while Kanam was neglected. He was forced to continue his quest for financial support so he could return to his beloved Africa and his true love: archaeology.

Soul Mates

Archaeology wasn't just Louis's true love. It was Mary's, too. When she joined Caton-Thompson at Louis's lecture at the Royal Anthropological Institute in London, Louis's and Mary's separate paths finally converged. As it turned out, Louis already knew about Mary because he'd seen the drawings she'd done for Liddell and Caton-Thompson. When he met her at the lecture, he asked her to draw for his upcoming book, *Adam's Ancestors*. She jumped at the chance to collaborate with him, drawing for his book in her spare time while she continued to dig for artifacts in England. Soon, Mary and Louis (who was still married to Frida) were seeing each other often, especially at archaeological meetings. After Louis and Frida separated in December 1933, Louis proposed to Mary. She said yes.

Scandal

Early 1934 was difficult for Louis and Mary as word spread of Louis's infidelity. Caton-Thompson, who was responsible for Mary's initial introduction to Louis at the Royal Anthropological Institute, was so furious with Mary for her relationship with Louis that the two women wouldn't speak again for another forty years. Cambridge University, where Louis lived and taught after separating from Frida, fired Louis. His peers looked down on him for his immoral behavior. The blow to his personal reputation also made it difficult for him to raise money for an excavation he wanted to start back in Africa, though he eventually raised enough to return for an expedition in October 1934. He arrived a few months ahead of the fateful visit from Percy Boswell, the scientist who criticized Leakey's work at Kanam.[1] Meanwhile, Mary stayed in England to finish her own excavation work.

Love Spell

When Mary joined Louis in Africa a couple years after his scandalous split from Frida and Boswell's stinging public attack, his troubles seemed to dim. He immediately brought her to his cherished Olduvai site. Mary's excitement about being in Africa didn't diminish during her first few days there, even when the going got tough: Their truck got stuck in mud several times, forcing them to unload their luggage and push the car, and they even had to sleep on a tarp on the ground in poor weather. A couple days in, she rose early on a clear morning and got a look at the Serengeti, where she saw thousands of animals. Africa had "cast its spell" on her.[2]

Louis had found his true partner.

It took only a few days for Mary to fall in love with Africa. The wild environment and sights of the Serengeti enchanted the young, curious woman.

A New Start

Louis's biggest find to date, the Kanam hominid, was full of tough lessons: He hadn't mapped the site, he hadn't photographed it thoroughly, he didn't have a geologist inspect and catalog the site, and his reputation was in tatters as a result. Upon his return to Olduvai, Louis began to be more meticulous about his work, mapping more than 100 miles (161 kilometers) of potential dig sites before starting excavations.

Meanwhile, Mary was getting acquainted with Africa as she, Louis, and Louis's excavation team set up camp at Olduvai during the summer of 1936. On a walk one day, she nearly tripped over a slumbering lion. Afraid, she ran away. The startled lion also ran away. On another walk, she encountered a rhinoceros. Still, she was charmed by her new surroundings, finding a familiar comfort in nature.

The summer digs at Olduvai failed to produce evidence of early hominids, although the team did find old tools and evidence of ancient animals and plants. The team was low on supplies, and Louis needed to raise money for continued work in Africa. He also had personal business to attend to back in England; when he and Mary returned to England in the fall of 1936, he divorced Frida.

Louis and Mary wed on Christmas Eve and were back in Kenya by early January 1937. They had some money from lectures Louis delivered during his time in England as well as an advance he received to write a book about the Kikuyu.[3]

An Unsettled Settlement

Though conflict between natives in British East Africa and the white settlers was infrequent, native tribes, including the Kikuyu, were rightfully resentful of the colonization that had taken their homes and the institutionalized segregation that made them

Kenya and the Brits

In the late nineteenth century, the powerful British Empire started colonizing what's now Kenya and some surrounding areas. By 1920, Britain had taken governmental control of the area, then called British East Africa, from the long-ruling Zanzibar Sultanate. Thousands of settlers from other British colonies—including Christian missionaries, such as Louis's parents—moved into the area. The colonization resulted in conflicts with native peoples such as the Kikuyu, who were forced from their homes so white settlers could have prime farmland. But Britain's might overpowered the scattered native tribes. The Kenya Colony was racially segregated to the disadvantage of nonwhite natives and settlers.[4] It was into this Kenya that Louis, the son of British settlers, was born.

socially inferior to the colonists. Still, as a young boy, Louis Leakey not only had managed to become friendly with the Kikuyu but had also been accepted as an honorary member of their tribe. Because of his relationship with them, the Kikuyu agreed to allow Louis to write a book about the tribe in 1937. The Kikuyu hoped Louis, a Brit who grew up with the Kikuyu, could bridge the gap between their tribe and the white settlers who controlled the territory. Louis spent early 1937 interviewing Kikuyu elders and soon had hundreds of pages for what would eventually be the "most complete record of a tribe" ever written.[5]

Unfortunately, bridging the gap between the Kikuyu and the white settlers would prove difficult. Louis was sympathetic to their situation, but he had little influence on the white settlers, who considered him a race traitor due to his friendship with the tribe.

Mary Digs In

While Louis worked on his book, Mary excavated. At the end of summer in 1937, they set up camp at a prehistoric site called Hyrax Hill in Kenya's Rift Valley. There, Mary found human

One of the first dig sites Mary and Louis Leakey started as a couple was in Kenya's Rift Valley, which yielded skeletons and artifacts dating back thousands of years.

skeletons that were a few hundred years old and some artifacts that dated back a couple thousand years. Word of her discoveries spread to other white settlers, most of whom thought Africa had little to offer in the way of history. Mary invited them to visit the Hyrax Hill camp. Hundreds showed up to view her artifacts. Many were shocked by the revelation that life in Africa extended far back into history. Some of the visitors gave Mary and Louis money to support the excavations, which was welcomed because the money Louis had gotten for the Kikuyu book had run out by 1939.[6]

The World Outside

Kenya had mostly been kept out of the fray of World War I, which was fought far away in mainland Europe. World War II would turn out to be a much different experience. When Italy, aligned with Adolf Hitler's Germany, invaded North Africa in 1939, the most brutal war in history edged toward Kenya's borders. As a member of the Allied powers (Hitler's opposition), Britain's government—even in Kenya—had to pour everything into the war. There was no way the Leakeys could appeal to the government for funding for their excavations, and there were no jobs for them in Kenya. To avoid having to return to England, Louis took a job with the British government's Special Branch. He was responsible for liaising with the native tribes and explaining Britain's involvement in the war. He was also charged with spying on the natives to find out if they planned to take advantage of Britain's preoccupation with the war to revolt against the British-controlled government in Kenya. As the war kicked into high gear, Louis began transporting weapons to Ethiopia, where Italy had invaded.[7]

The couple's archaeological work came to a halt as they faced the new realities imposed by World War II. Their wild sanctuary

When Italy invaded North Africa in World War II, the war came to Kenya's front door. The conflict disrupted the Leakeys' work, and resources were rerouted to the war effort.

was threatened by the global hostilities. British by birth but Kenyan at heart, Louis faced conflicting loyalties. The future was uncertain.

CHAPTER FOUR

Rising from the Rubble

As World War II consumed Europe and northern Africa in 1940, Louis and Mary's life was uprooted. They lacked funds to maintain their camp in the Rift Valley. They moved to Kenya's capital city, Nairobi. Although the war had disrupted the work they loved, they weren't going to let it threaten what they'd accomplished. They hauled their piles of archaeological findings to Nairobi, where—thanks to Louis's government job—they were allowed to store their precious objects at the Coryndon Museum. The government also gave them a dilapidated house to live in.[1]

In 1940, Britain was fully engaged in World War II against Germany and Italy. That summer, Britain battled Italy as the latter advanced into British East Africa.

Growing Pains

Amid these hostilities, Louis and Mary's first child, Jonathan, was born in November 1940. Unfortunately, Louis was often away, working on behalf of Britain. When he was home, Louis and Mary brought baby Jonathan on digs, even bringing him to Louis's most cherished site, Olduvai.

In 1940—just as World War II began to rage across several continents—the Leakeys' first son, Jonathan (pictured here at his Kenyan snake farm in 1972), was born.

In April 1943, the Leakeys' second child, Deborah, died just a few months after she was born. Grief-stricken, Louis and Mary suspended their beloved, if sporadic, archaeological work. Louis worked long days on behalf of the British government and volunteered nights at the museum, where Mary also logged a lot of volunteer hours.[2]

Despite their personal hardships and the pressures of the war, Louis and Mary continued to collaborate in archaeological work whenever they could. In 1942, they began digging at a dry lake bed south of Nairobi where they found artifacts such as hand axes and other tools. Unfortunately, they had little time to spend at the site. Louis had hoped to find evidence of very early humans there, but the Leakeys didn't find anything particularly earth-shattering. Still, their finds at the lake bed in 1942 had generated interest in the site. Scientists from around the world started visiting Kenya and the rest of the continent in search for evidence of ancient peoples.[3]

Delayed Dreams

The Leakeys took an interest in digging on Rusinga Island in 1942, but their work there was put on hold when, in 1943, World War II took another turn that threatened Africa. Italy had been driven out of Africa, but a new Axis threat, Japan, sent submarines to scout the Kenyan coast. For two years, Louis was dispatched to investigate this new threat on behalf of the British government. While looking into this threat, he learned that resentful African natives were aiding Japan and Germany with supplies and information about British war plans. Amid this chaos, Mary gave birth to a second son, Richard, in December 1944.[4]

The war ended in 1945, but Louis had to continue working for the Special Branch to make money. When the Kenyan government was able to free up public funds again, Louis was hired as the

Proconsul

In 1942 and 1943, the Leakeys began digging on Rusinga Island ("Island of the Apes") in Lake Victoria. An ancient volcanic eruption had covered Rusinga in ash, which helped preserve fossils. On a 1943 trip to Rusinga, Louis found the jaw of a *Proconsul*, an ancestor of modern apes and humans that lived about twenty-five million years ago. The jaw still had all its teeth on one side and provided valuable evolutionary insight into the *Proconsul* skeletal structure.[5] It was a significant find. However, it merely scratched the surface of Rusinga's treasures—discoveries that would have to wait until the war was over.

On Kenya's Rusinga Island (with Lake Victoria pictured in the distance), the Leakeys found a *Proconsul* fossil, preserved in volcanic ash, that dated back twenty-five million years.

In 1944, the Leakeys' second son, Richard (pictured here in 1977 with skull discoveries), was born. At the time, World War II still raged and native unrest in Kenya was rising.

curator of the Coryndon Museum, where he and Mary had volunteered for five years and stored their archaeological finds.

Postwar Woes

After the war, disgruntled Kenyan natives formed a terrorist group to reclaim their homeland. Tensions were high between the natives and the white settlers in still-segregated Kenya. Meanwhile, England, was in bad shape. When Mary traveled there with her sons in the spring of 1946 to visit her ailing mother, she found London a pile of rubble after years of bombings.[6] Her mother died within two weeks of her arrival. After the funeral, Mary and her young sons were stuck in England for about six months because of a shortage of passenger ships.[7]

In Kenya, Louis, who spoke some native languages as well as English, was increasingly caught in the middle of hostile interactions and negotiations between the natives and the white settlers. Mary was forced to face the toll the war had taken on England and its people. Things looked bleak.

Louis Takes the Lead

Separated from his family, Louis focused on returning to archaeological work and on his new job as museum curator. At the museum, Louis did more than just oversee operations and exhibits—he made the museum's rules. He used this power to desegregate the museum in a country where segregation was routine.[8] White people who had settled in Kenya held the political power and ranked at the top of the social order. Louis, who'd grown up as a friend to the native Kikuyu tribe, had never agreed with the racial segregation in Kenya. He and Mary regularly collaborated with natives in excavations, recognizing the value of their firsthand knowledge of the region. So, under Louis's management, people of color were able to view the museum's exhibits alongside white people for the first time. With this directive, Louis became a sociopolitical leader as well as a scientist. It wouldn't be the last time he or a member of his family rebuffed the political and social norms of white-controlled Kenya.

The Ultimate Collaboration

Rather than going to retrieve Mary and his children from England in 1946, Louis stayed in Africa because he was deep into planning something big: a Pan-African Congress on Prehistory.

Recent findings across Africa were giving scientists pause about the birthplace of modern human beings and the prevailing "Out of Asia" theory. Louis recognized the need to bring together scientists so they could collaborate on a consensus about the age of African fossils.

Louis, who was still haunted by the Kanam embarrassment, also hoped the congress would salvage his career and reputation. While he planned this big event, he began showing journalists his archaeological finds, despite pressure from his peers to keep his findings confined to scientific journals until peer review could substantiate the often lofty claims Louis made about his discoveries. Louis found he liked the publicity, which gave him some measure of celebrity and attracted investors.[9] As news of the congress spread, scientists involved in African excavations agreed to participate.

Reunion and Recognition

Though planning for the congress was all-consuming, other members believed Louis needed to go to the aid of his wife and children, who were stranded in England for much of 1946. They gave him money to travel there. They had, of course, an ulterior motive: to get Louis to invite scientists in London to the Pan-African Congress. Louis spent most of his time in England visiting scientists and universities. In October, the Leakeys finally returned to Nairobi, and the next three months were spent feverishly preparing for the January 1947 congress.

The first Pan-African Congress on Prehistory was so successful that members agreed to meet every four years. Louis got credit for bringing the group together for a much-needed conversation about Africa's place in human evolutionary history. For his efforts, Louis received the scientific and professional praise he so desperately wanted.

At the first Pan-African Congress on Prehistory, the usually quiet and reserved Mary Leakey—who had no formal education—was recognized by scientific peers for her paleoanthropological achievements.

Mary, too, benefited from attending the event. Usually quiet, reserved, and uncomfortable in the spotlight, the congress meeting forced Mary to come out of her shell. She spoke about her own archaeological work and was pleased to find the congress members were impressed with her accomplishments.[10] Mary was no longer just a shadow behind Louis; her years of collaborating with her husband had proved her own worth to others in the profession.

Things were finally looking up for the Leakeys.

CHAPTER FIVE

Family and Fame

With World War II and the first Pan-African Congress behind them, the Leakeys wanted to start over. The event had elevated their profile in the scientific community and restored Louis's reputation. It had also attracted the attention of investors who provided financial support for the Leakeys' excavations. The Kenyan government and the British Royal Society subsidized the Leakeys' work.[1] For the first time, Louis and Mary could breathe a little easier as they looked to the future.

As the dust settled in early 1947, Mary, Louis, and their two sons got to be together as a family. Because of Louis's museum job, they stayed in Nairobi, settling into a house that was always packed full of fossils, excavation tools, and animals—everything from mice to snakes to a pony.[2]

Excavations were a family affair for the Leakeys, as evidenced by this photo of the Leakey family inspecting the campsite of an early hominid at Olduvai Gorge in Tanzania.

The Return to Rusinga

The Leakeys' priority was to return to the island of Rusinga in Lake Victoria. Rusinga was a fossil gold mine; ancient life there was preserved when a volcano exploded ash across the island about twenty million years ago.[3]

By the end of 1947, the Leakey team unearthed more than thirteen hundred fossils, including teeth, jaws, and palates of ancient apes, as well as other ancient animal and insect fossils. These fossils gave the Leakey team a picture of ancient life on Rusinga, where apes coexisted with everything from small insects to elephants to crocodiles (which still lived in Lake Victoria at the time of the excavation). Traces of plant life also informed the team about what grew on Rusinga all those millions of years ago.[4]

The Leakeys raced to find something big before other excavators arrived. The fossils they'd already found on Rusinga led them to believe the island could offer something truly groundbreaking.

Mary's Big Find

In September 1948, Mary unearthed a *Proconsul* jaw with its teeth on Rusinga. She yelled for Louis to join her, and together, they dug around the jaw to reveal it buried with part of its skull. Over the next few days, Louis and Mary painstakingly excavated around the site until they found all the skull's scraps of bone, which Mary fitted together. When she was finished, she and Louis were the first people living to look into the full face of a *Proconsul*. This was a major find—*Proconsul* was an ape that had lived twenty million years ago.[5]

Proconsul africanus

In 1948, Mary found a *Proconsul* skull on Rusinga. It was so small that she could hold it in the palm of her hand. After days of hard labor looking for every tiny piece of the skull Mary had unearthed with Louis, they got to see the ancient creature's features: the structure of its jaw, its forehead, its eye sockets. For serious paleoanthropologists like Mary and Louis, looking into the face of the *Proconsul africanus* (the scientific name given to the hominoid Mary had found) was a life-changing experience. Finding it together after a carefully collaborated dig made the discovery even more special. Later in life, Mary would recall that she and Louis were "exhilarated and also utterly content with each other" upon making the discovery as a team.[6]

Louis—ever the overeager explorer—was convinced he and his wife had found the skull of an early human ancestor.

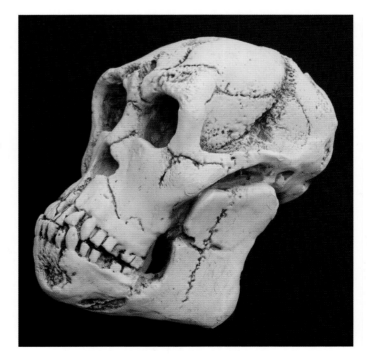

The *Proconsul africanus* skull found by Mary Leakey at Rusinga was a major find. The skull dated back thirty-four to twenty-three million years and had some human-like features.

He thought the finished skull looked more like a human skull than that of an ape. Louis photographed the skull for his friends in England, who shared them with journalists. The Leakeys' discovery was soon published all over the news, and speculation about whether the skull belonged to an early human ancestor ran wild.

Everyone wanted a look at the *Proconsul africanus*. As the discoverer of the skull, Mary got the honor of bringing it to London for a press junket. An airline let her fly to London for free so she could share her discovery with the press and with the Leakeys' expert friends. She packed the skull with care and held it close the entire flight to England.

Shy, quiet Mary was mobbed by curious onlookers and reporters the moment she stepped off the plane in London. Many people were interested that it was Mary and not her boastful, Cambridge-educated husband who'd found the skull. After meeting with the press, she brought the skull to Oxford University for further analysis. After a two-week analysis, an Oxford expert determined the skull was not the evidence of an early human ancestor that Louis had hoped it was. Its nose and muzzle resembled monkeys, while the jaw area resembled apes. So, while the skull wasn't a link to an early human ancestor, it was a link between apes and monkeys.[7] This gave the finding significance, even if it wasn't the answer Louis had wanted.

A Famous Family

The assessment of the skull was printed in stories around the world. Curious people swarmed the British Museum of Natural History to see the skull Mary had found. The Leakeys were officially famous. Money poured in to support their work. More good fortune came to the Leakeys in June 1949 with the birth of their third son, Philip.

In 1949, the Leakeys' son Philip was born. Pictured here with members of the native Maasai, Philip served in the Kenyan Parliament from 1979 to 1992.

Fame and money didn't change the family. Louis, inspired by his own youth in Kenya, brought his sons on nature walks. He taught them to make tools, build fires, and get near wild animals without being noticed. New "pets" were brought to the family home all the time, especially as the boys began bringing home any wild animal they could get their hands on. This menagerie resulted in an interesting twist for the Leakey family: The sons appreciated living animals far more than the fossils that dominated their parents' lives. In fact, none of the boys showed clear signs that they'd follow in their parents' professional steps.

Time would tell.

CHAPTER SIX

A Whole New World

Following the headlining discovery of the *Proconsul africanus* skull and the success of the inaugural Pan-African Congress of Prehistory, the Leakeys' lives changed forever. While Louis continued routine work like managing the Coryndon Museum, writing scientific papers and books, and negotiating between rebellious natives and the British government, he worked alongside Mary to organize the second Pan-African Congress on Prehistory. But, true to the Leakeys' way, it was their archaeological finds that would continue to captivate the world.

Olduvai

Louis had revered the Olduvai Gorge since his first excavations there in the 1930s. The tumultuous 1940s had prevented the Leakeys from continuing to explore the gorge, which lies about 295 miles (474 km) southwest of Nairobi in present-day Tanzania. Louis insisted they'd find an early human at Olduvai, so the family set up camp there in 1951.

First Finds

On earlier trips to Olduvai, Louis and Mary had found rudimentary tools in lower beds and hand axes in higher beds, which showed progressive intelligence among the early humans who'd made them. On the 1951 trip, Mary and Louis found animal remains among stone tools, which the Leakeys believed an ancient tribe used to cut up the animals for food. Firmly believing their next big breakthrough would be at Olduvai, Mary and Louis maintained excavation sites there throughout the 1950s.[1]

During school breaks, Jonathan and Richard would visit Olduvai, where Louis continued their education in nature and fossils.[2] Philip, only two years old, lived at the site with Louis and Mary. World famous or not, the Leakey family was just as focused on its work—and the unique way of life that work resulted in—as they were before they made international news headlines.

The Big Break

The Leakeys' Olduvai work attracted the attention of a Kenyan television show called *On Safari*. The show's producers wanted to film the excavation, arriving on site July 17, 1959.[3] They were right on time. Although Louis felt too ill to leave camp that day, Mary was about to make another incredible find.

After an uneventful morning, Mary found a large piece of a hominid skull containing some teeth. She ran back to camp, where she rallied her husband with cries of "I've got him!"

Louis and Mary ran back to where she'd found the skull, waiting until the cameras arrived to continue digging. Louis contemplated the skull; its features resembled an australopithecine, a near-man species of undetermined age whose fossils had been found in South Africa. Some scientists believed australopithecine was a direct human ancestor; Louis disagreed, believing a different apelike creature had survived natural selection to become the human ancestor. Another consideration was that experts didn't think the australopithecine possessed the intelligence to make tools, but the skull Mary found was near stone tools. Had Mary found a previously undiscovered species, or even the skull of a very early human?

Over the next nineteen days, with photographers on site, the Leakeys painstakingly excavated the skull's fragments and pieced it together. They were still unsure if the skull had belonged to a human ancestor. Believing it to be a new species, Louis called it Zinjanthropus ("Man from East Africa," also known as "Zinj") and packed it in a cookie tin.[4] Luckily, the fourth Pan-African Congress was happening the next month. There, scientists argued over the significance of Zinj and over Louis's theory that he'd found a new species that lived between five hundred thousand and one million years ago.

"Dear Boy"

Due to the geological layer in which the skull was found, experts concluded Zinj (whom Louis called "Dear Boy") was much older than earlier estimates: 1.75 million years old.

Zinj was a newly found species, *Paranthropus boisei*. Later research revealed this species may have lived as far back as 2.3 million years and existed for about 1.1 million years (four times longer than *Homo sapiens* have existed). Though it's not a direct human ancestor, Zinj is a member of the human lineage, or "fossil hominin," and probably lived alongside human ancestors.[5]

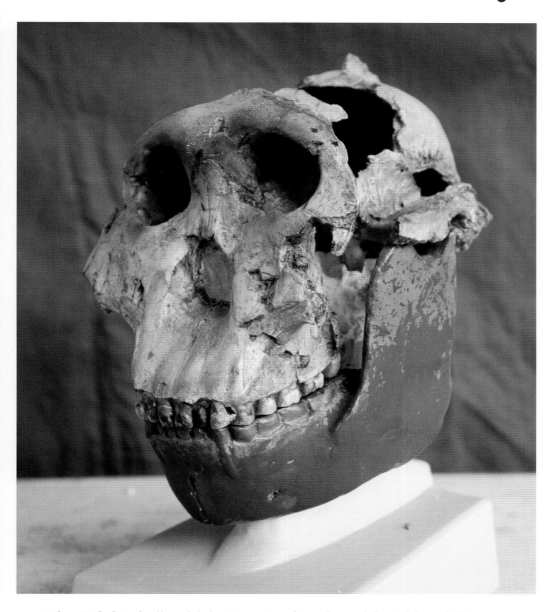

The "Zinj" skull, which Mary Leakey found in Olduvai Gorge, was a newly found species that dated back between one and two million years and probably lived among human ancestors.

A Family Affair

Zinj was international news. Louis embarked on a tour of the United States and England, giving speeches and displaying the skull in lecture halls overflowing with curious people. Louis loved the spotlight and fame. Olduvai was no longer a quiet, family-run excavation site, but the focus of intense international attention. Luckily, the money Louis made from his Zinj lectures allowed the Leakeys to begin another Olduvai excavation in early 1960.

Mary's Charge

Between his lecture tours and Coryndon Museum duties, Louis could spend very little time at the new excavation site. Mary assumed full control over the 1960 excavation—the first of many times she'd manage a dig—with help from her oldest son, Jonathan (and the five pet dogs that followed her everywhere).

For the 1960 Olduvai dig, the Leakeys brought on an almost entirely new crew, many of whom hadn't worked for the family before—and many of whom had never taken orders from a woman. Mary overcame these challenges by working with the crew, using heavy tools and getting dirty alongside them, and by teaching them her meticulous digging style. They respected her enough to follow her rule of no talking or singing while they worked, acknowledging that those distractions could cause a person to miss the sometimes minuscule pieces of bone that were often part of a bigger picture.[6] Mary, who had no formal education and was essentially a self-taught scientist in a male-dominated industry, was in command of the most famous dig site in the world.

Throughout 1960, the Leakeys and their team found the bones of a female hominid; the jawbone of a saber-toothed tiger (which had never before been found in East Africa), and a Zinj

Mary Leakey didn't just make groundbreaking finds—she also succeeded in a male-dominated scientific field by commanding the respect of her teams and teaching them her meticulous excavation methods.

living floor—essentially, a campsite where the remains of the species' daily activities were centralized. In August 1960, Mary became the first person to ever find foot bones belonging to an early bipedal hominid. She and Louis found more fossils about 1 foot (30.5 centimeters) below the living floor, which belonged to a hominid that lived several thousand years before Zinj.[7]

Johnny's Child

Throughout the fall of 1960, twenty-year-old Jonathan found fragments of an adolescent-aged child's skull, a finger, and hand

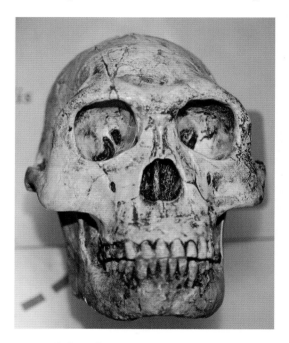

and wrist bones. Because the bones obviously belonged to a young hominid, they were nicknamed "Johnny's Child." Johnny's Child was almost two million years old. It had a bigger cranium than Zinj. Its hand bones indicated it had a precision grip, in which the thumb and other fingers could touch each other. After collaborating with paleoanthropologist Phillip Tobias for three years in the study of Johnny's Child, the Leakeys concluded Johnny's Child and his contemporaries had made the stone tools they'd found at Olduvai. Even more significant was Tobias's confirmation that Johnny's Child was closer to

Found by the Leakeys' oldest son, Jonathan, skeletal fragments of "Johnny's Child" indicated the nearly two-million-year-old hominid had human-like characteristics, like a precision grip.

a *Homo* than was Zinj.[8] Johnny's Child was the earliest member of *Homo habilis*, a scientific name meaning "Handy Man."

In November 1960, Jonathan found a lower jaw with big front teeth and small rear teeth (the Zinj had small front teeth and large back teeth). With the jaw discovery, Jonathan proved wrong the many scientists who believed different types of hominids hadn't coexisted.[9]

The next generation of Leakeys had arrived.

CHAPTER SEVEN

Launching a Legacy

As the 1960s rolled on, the Leakeys' fame grew as news of their findings was published worldwide. Louis threw himself into new ventures, including opening an African prehistory center at the Coryndon Museum and making a movie about ancient life. Content to stay out of the spotlight, Mary kept up the Olduvai work. The Leakey sons helped their mother manage and excavate at Olduvai. At just twelve years old, Philip excavated a living floor at Olduvai that was two million years old.[1]

Divergent Paths

As word of Johnny's Child traveled, Louis traveled with it, bringing the fossil to lectures around the world. He also started excavations in Israel and in Calico, California (which would turn up nothing after six years of digging and serve as Louis's final humiliation). He stepped outside his family to further his legacy by training three young women in the study of wild animals: Jane Goodall and Biruté Galdikas, primatologists and anthropologists, and Dian Fossey, a primatologist. Nicknamed the "Trimates" or "Leakey's Angels," all three would eventually achieve global fame for their groundbreaking work with primates.[2] Louis's endeavors left Mary and their sons to handle things back home.

Jonathan and Philip drifted away from the family's paleoanthropology work but stayed in East Africa. Jonathan went into business selling snake venoms and plants for medicinal purposes. Philip went into politics, serving as a member of the Kenyan Parliament from 1979 to 1992, before starting an export business. After dropping out of high school, Richard undertook various endeavors, including becoming a pilot, starting a safari business, and marrying and divorcing archaeologist Margaret Cropper within six years.

A Labored Legacy

By the late 1960s, Louis was almost seventy and in poor health. He never let this slow him down; even at home, he worked on scientific literature. Eventually, he had to give up his travels and oversight of his projects. Since the discoveries of Zinj and Johnny's Child, Louis was always on the go, barely seeing his family. His oldest and youngest sons strayed from the family business. His relationships with Mary and Richard became strained; he and Mary separated in the late 1960s, while Richard's rebelliousness put distance between father and son. While the Leakeys had grown famous, the family had been falling apart.

Richard, the family's most unlikely candidate, became the son who would carry on the family's paleoanthropological work. He took over Louis's position at the Coryndon Museum in the late 1960s. In 1970, he married paleontologist Meave Epps and, with her, settled into the life he'd been raised to live. By the early 1970s, Richard was leading his own expeditions. On his 1972 expedition at Lake Turkana (formerly Lake Rudolf, in eastern Africa), Richard found parts of a hominid skull in soil dating back 2.6 million years, which Meave helped him reconstruct.[3]

Richard Leakey's wife Meave Epps, a paleontologist, has helped carry the Leakey legacy into the twenty-first century by leading her own expeditions.

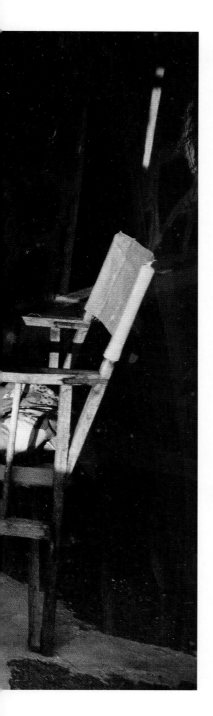

One Last Look

In September 1972, Louis was about to travel to London. For nearly forty years, Louis had contended a creature like *Homo erectus* had existed in Africa two million years ago, and he'd spent much of his life seeking it. In late September, Richard and his mother flew to Nairobi with the evidence: skull 1470. Louis was delighted. He praised Richard, who'd found a fossil that validated an old theory and reconciled father and son.

A few days later, Louis died of a heart attack in London. Mary later recalled that Louis was "excited, triumphant, sublimely happy" during that last meeting, when the family's chief paleoanthropologists did what they loved most: study an amazing family find.[4]

Named after its field number, 1470, the skull was the largest early hominid skull ever found and big enough for a *Homo erectus* brain.[5]

Louis's death on October 1, 1972, was international news, and dignitaries, scientists from around the world, and his Kikuyu friends attended his funeral

In the late 1970s, Mary Leakey found ancient footprints on the Laetoli Plain in Tanzania. The footprints had been preserved by volcanic ash and dated back about three million years.

in Kenya. The Leakey legacy was left to Louis's family, who returned to work shortly after his funeral.

Moving On

With Louis gone, Mary had to begin making the public appearances her husband had always jumped at. She traveled around the world, giving lectures and going to scientific symposiums, including the 1977 Pan-African Congress—the congress she and her husband had started thirty years prior. She received awards and recognition, but was still happiest doing her excavation work, which she continued at Olduvai.

In 1976, Mary moved to Laetoli, which was about 30 miles (48 km) from Olduvai. Laetoli was a volcanic ash–covered site where she'd been digging for two years. There, she found bipedal footprints, including some resembling human feet, that had hardened in the ash.[6] The ash helped Mary date the footprints at about 3.5 million years old. She had made an incredible discovery; not only did these very ancient creatures walk upright, they "were doing it much earlier than nearly everyone supposed and without the big brains long considered necessary for bipedalism."[7] In 1977, Mary found footprint tracks that indicated a hominid family (a male, a female, and a child) had passed through, perhaps during a volcanic eruption. This story enchanted the world. Mary called it "perhaps the most remarkable find" of her entire career.[8]

After finding the Laetoli tracks, Mary moved back to Olduvai, where she wrote and studied her findings. In 1982, at age seventy, Mary went blind in one eye. She moved into the family house near Nairobi, where she continued to write, attend scientific meetings, and spend time with her family. When Mary died in December 1996, the world mourned the loss of a woman who'd made some of the family's—and science's—most profound discoveries.[9]

Richard: From Reluctant Child to Scientist, Politician, and Activist

Richard and Meave became the principal scientists of the Leakey family following Mary's death, continuing to research human origins in East Africa. Leading fossil hunters known as the "Hominid Gang," Richard and his teams spent decades unearthing ancient fossils.[10] In 1989, Richard was appointed to lead the Kenya Wildlife Services; ever since, he's fought to conserve Kenya's wildlife and to stop poaching. When a 1993

Richard Leakey has dedicated his life to the preservation of Africa's wildlife and the fight against poaching. He's pictured here in 2006 examining elephant tusks buried by poachers in Kenya.

airplane accident resulted in below-the-knee amputations on both his legs, Richard gave up excavation work but continued his political and conservation work and learned to walk using prostheses. In the 1990s, he was appointed to the Kenyan Parliament, and he remains active in the country's politics.[11] In 2002, he took an anthropology professorship at Stony Brook University in New York, and in 2004, he founded WildlifeDirect, a global organization dedicated to conservation in Kenya.[12]

Conclusion

Meave, who is also a research professor at Stony Brook, kept up the Leakey tradition of excavation. In 1995, she found a bipedal hominid species that was four million years old. In 2001, she announced that her team—including her twenty-eight-year-old daughter Louise, who has a doctorate in biology from University College, London—found a new genus and species of human ancestor, *Kenyanthropus platyop*.[1] Louise, who has been digging for fossils since she was a little girl, and Meave are National Geographic "Explorers-in-Residence," scientists who collaborate with National Geographic to make discoveries.[2] Like her parents, Louise is a Stony Brook professor. She also helps direct the Turkana Basin Institute, set up in 2005 by Richard and Stony Brook to ensure year-round research in the East Africa region of Turkana Basin. In 2015, Louise, a 3D printing and digital pioneer in her field, partnered with software company Autodesk to create 3D replicas of fossils as old as three million years. These replicas help this modern Leakey share "fascinating evidence of human evolution with people around the world."[3] With her husband, Prince Emmanuel de Merode, a Belgian primatologist and high-

Richard and Meave's oldest daughter, Louise (*left*), has followed the Leakey family legacy by becoming a world-renowned paleontologist and continuing excavation and preservation work in Africa.

profile conservationist, Louise has two daughters, Princesses Seiyia, born in 2004, and Alexia, born in 2006.

Merode has personally intervened to save endangered and at-risk wildlife in Africa while Louise continues the paleoanthropology work of her grandparents. Though the work they do looks different than the hands-on excavation work of Louis and Mary, Richard, Meave, Louise, and Merode carry on the Leakey legacy of discovery—work that the family's been doing for nearly one hundred years. Richard and Louise have enriched the Leakey legacy through important work such as conservation, political involvement, and collaborating through international and academic partnerships, ensuring their work can be carried on by future generations of scientists.

Louise's husband, Prince Emmanuel de Merode, is a prima-tologist and conservationist who intervenes on behalf of African wildlife threatened by poachers and by civil unrest that disturbs African wildlife ecosystems.

The contribution of the Leakey family to the world is difficult to measure. They're special for their fossil discoveries, for the insight their finds provided into human evolution, and for generating widespread interest in the study of human origins. Through endeavors such as training the Trimates, the Leakeys' special brand of hands-on scientific discovery was passed on through the work and findings of other preeminent scientists. However, what really sets the Leakeys apart from other scientists can be described in one word: family. Beginning with the collaboration of Mary and Louis, the Leakey family has created a scientific dynasty whose members tirelessly champion discovery, learning, and protecting wildlife and precious natural resources. Their work has firmly entrenched the Leakeys in the annals of scientists who changed the world. The First Family of Paleontology is proof that collaboration can take many forms, and through collaboration, unbelievable achievements are possible.

CHRONOLOGY

- **1903** Louis Leakey is born on August 7 in Kenya to Christian missionary parents from England.

- **1913** Mary Nicol is born February 6 in London, England.

- **1927** Louis begins his first Kenyan expedition.

- **1932** Louis starts an excavation at Kanam and Olduvai and meets Mary in London.

- **1935** Percy Boswell visits Kanam and publishes a scathing criticism of Louis.

- **1936** Louis and Frida divorce; Louis and Mary wed on December 24.

- **1939** World War II begins.

- **1940** Son Jonathan is born on November 4.

- **1943** Daughter Deborah is born and dies a few months later.

- **1944** Son Richard is born on December 19.

- **1945** World War II ends.

- **1948** Mary discovers a *Proconsul africanus* skull.

- **1949** Son Philip is born on June 21.

- **1959** *Zinjanthropus boisei* skull is discovered.

- **1960** Johnny's Child is discovered.

- **1963** *Homo habilis* is discovered.

- **1967** Richard forms Kenya Museum Associates.

- **1970** Louis has a heart attack; Richard marries paleoanthropologist Meave Epps.

- **1972** Richard discovers a 2.6-million-year-old *Homo* skull; Louis dies on October 1.

- **1973** Richard and Meave's daughter Louise, a future paleo-anthropologist, is born on March 21.

- **1978** Mary discovers Laetoli footprints.

- **1984** The Leakey team discovers Turkana Boy.

- **1989** Richard is appointed head of Kenya's Wildlife Conservation and Management Department.

- **1993** Louise joins Meave as coleader of paleontological expeditions in Kenya.

- **1994** Meave's team discovers a four-million-year-old *Australopithecus anamensis* in Ethiopia.

- **1996** Mary dies on December 9.

- **2004** Richard founds WildlifeDirect to support African conservationists.

CHAPTER NOTES

Introduction

1. Stony Brook University, "Five Questions with Richard Leakey," You Tube, posted October 27, 2016, https://youtu.be/eMgd6b1zsg0.

Chapter One 🔬 Origins

1. Richard G. Klein, "Darwin and the Recent African Origin of Modern Humans," PNAS, September 22, 2009, https://www.pnas.org/content/106/38/16007.
2. History.com Editors, "*Origin of Species* Is Published," History, November 24, 2009, https://www.history.com/this-day-in-history/origin-of-species-is-published-2.
3. Riley Black, "What's a 'Missing Link'?" *Smithsonian Magazine*, March 6, 2018, https://www.smithsonianmag.com/science-nature/whats-missing-link-180968327.
4. Garniss H. Curtis, Roger Lewin, and Carl C. Swisher, *Java Man: How Two Geologists Changed Our Understanding of Human Evolution* (Chicago: The University of Chicago Press, 2000), pp. 66–67.
5. Virginia Morell, *Ancestral Passions: The Leakey Family and the Quest for Humankind's Beginnings* (New York: Simon & Schuster, 1995), p. 23.
6. Margaret Poynter, *The Leakeys: Uncovering the Origins of Humankind* (Springfield, NJ: Enslow Publishers, 1997), p. 17.
7. Poynter, pp. 16–17.
8. Poynter, pp. 17–20.
9. Poynter, p. 28.

Chapter Two 🔬 Parallel Paths

1. Margaret Poynter, *The Leakeys: Uncovering the Origins of Humankind* (Springfield, NJ: Enslow Publishers, 1997), pp. 20–21.
2. Poynter, p. 22.
3. Poynter, pp. 24–25.
4. Poynter, p. 26.

5. Poynter, p. 29.
6. Deborah Heiligman, *Mary Leakey: In Search of Human Beginnings* (New York: Goodreads Press, 1994), "Chapter 2: An Adventure Growing Up," Kindle Location 151.
7. Heiligman, "Chapter 3: A Bit of a Bang," Kindle Locations 174–175.
8. Heiligman, "Chapter 3: A Bit of a Bang," Kindle Locations 178, 193, 197.
9. Heiligman, "Chapter 3: A Bit of a Bang," Kindle Locations 201–202.

Chapter Three ✳ True Love and Tumult

1. Mary Bowman-Kruhm, *The Leakeys: A Biography* (Westport, CT: Greenwood Press, 2005), p. 29.
2. Mary Leakey, *Disclosing the Past* (Garden City, NY: Doubleday, 1984), p. 63.
3. Margaret Poynter, *The Leakeys: Uncovering the Origins of Humankind* (Springfield, NJ: Enslow Publishers, 1997), p. 32.
4. Maina Kiarie, "British East Africa Protectorate," Enzi Museum, http://www.enzimuseum.org/after-the-stone-age/british-east-africa-protectorate (accessed February 3, 2019).
5. Poynter, p. 33.
6. Poynter, pp. 35–36.
7. Poynter, pp. 36–37.

Chapter Four ✳ Rising from the Rubble

1. Margaret Poynter, *The Leakeys: Uncovering the Origins of Humankind* (Springfield, NJ: Enslow Publishers, 1997), p. 38.
2. Poynter, pp. 39–40.
3. Poynter, p. 40.
4. Mary Leakey, *Disclosing the Past* (Garden City, NY: Doubleday, 1984), p. 89.
5. Poynter, pp. 39–42

6. Virginia Morell, *Ancestral Passions: The Leakey Family and the Quest for Humankind's Beginnings* (New York: Simon & Schuster, 1995), p. 138.
7. Poynter, p. 45.
8. Poynter, p. 43.
9. Morell, p. 142.
10. Poynter, pp. 45–47.

Chapter Five ☸ Family and Fame

1. Margaret Poynter, *The Leakeys: Uncovering the Origins of Humankind* (Springfield, NJ: Enslow Publishers, 1997), p. 48.
2. Poynter, p. 55.
3. Poynter, p. 49.
4. Poynter, pp. 50–51.
5. Mary Leakey, *Disclosing the Past* (Garden City, NY: Doubleday, 1984), pp. 98–99.
6. Virginia Morell, *Ancestral Passions: The Leakey Family and the Quest for Humankind's Beginnings* (New York: Simon & Schuster, 1995), p. 150.
7. Poynter, pp. 53–54.

Chapter Six ☸ A Whole New World

1. Margaret Poynter, *The Leakeys: Uncovering the Origins of Humankind* (Springfield, NJ: Enslow Publishers, 1997), pp. 61–63.
2. Virginia Morell, *Ancestral Passions: The Leakey Family and the Quest for Humankind's Beginnings* (New York: Simon & Schuster, 1995), p. 158.
4. Poynter, pp. 64–67.
5. "*Paranthropus boisei*," Smithsonian National Museum of Natural History, http://humanorigins.si.edu/evidence/human-fossils/species/paranthropus-boisei (accessed April 1, 2019).
6. Morell, p. 201.
7. Poynter, pp. 76–78.
8. Morell, p. 234.

9. Poynter, pp. 77–78.

Chapter Seven ⚛ Launching a Legacy

1. Margaret Poynter, *The Leakeys: Uncovering the Origins of Humankind* (Springfield, NJ: Enslow Publishers, 1997), pp. 81–85.
2. Virginia Morell, "Called 'Trimates,' Three Bold Women Shaped Their Field," *Science*, April 16, 1993, pp. 420–425.
3. Poynter, p. 91.
4. Mary Leakey, *Disclosing the Past* (Garden City, NY: Doubleday, 1984), p. 159.
5. "KNM-ER 1470," Smithsonian National Museum of Natural History, http://humanorigins.si.edu/evidence/human-fossils/fossils/knm-er-1470 (accessed February 10, 2019).
6. Poynter, pp. 99–102.
7. Frederic Golden, "First Lady of Fossils," *Time*, December 23, 1996, p. 33.
8. Roger Lewin, *Bones of Contention* (New York: Simon and Schuster, 1987), p. 150.
9. Poynter, pp. 105–107.
10. Virginia Morell, "Richard Leakey," *Smithsonian Magazine*, November 1, 2005, https://www.smithsonianmag.com/science-nature/35-who-made-a-difference-richard-leakey-114600436.
11. "Richard Leakey," Leakey.com, http://www.leakey.com/bios/richard-leakey (accessed February 1, 2019).
12. Brian Smith, "The First Family of Paleoanthropology," *Stony Brook University Magazine*, Spring 2016, https://www.stonybrook.edu/magazine/2016-spring/the-first-family-of-paleoanthropology.

Conclusion

1. "Meave Leakey," Leakey.com, http://www.leakey.com/bios/meave-leakey (accessed February 1, 2019).

2. Stuart Thornton, "Paleontologist: Dr. Louise Leakey," *National Geographic,* April 4, 2012, https://www.national geographic.org/news/real-world-geography-louise-leakey.
3. Debra Thimmesch, "Autodesk & Dr. Louise Leakey Share 3.3-Million-Year-Old Stone Tools with the World via 3D Printing," 3DPrint.com, May 28, 2015, https://3dprint.com/68226/memento-ancient-tools.

GLOSSARY

anthropology The biological study of humans, early hominids, and primates, and the cultural, social, and linguistic study of humans.

archaeology The study of human history and prehistory through excavation and study of artifacts.

australopithecine A near-man species whose fossils were from an undetermined time period.

bipedalism The first step in the development of modern humans, the process by which humans and their ancestors walked upright instead of on all fours.

evolution The change over multiple generations of a species, based on natural selection.

excavation The exposure, processing, and recording of archaeological remains.

genus A rank in the biological classification of both living and fossil organisms.

geology The science of Earth's physical structure and history.

hominid A biological family group that includes humans, their ancestors, and some great apes.

hominoid A primate group that includes humans, their fossil ancestors, and anthropoid apes (apes with human forms).

Homo A genus of the hominid family (primates) characterized by features such as a large cranium and bipedalism.

Homo sapiens The only still-surviving human species.

natural selection A biological process in which some organisms
adapt better to their environment and therefore survive
and procreate, whereas those who don't adapt die off and
go extinct.

paleoanthropology A branch of anthropology dealing with
fossil hominids.

paleontology The science of fossil animals and plants and the
geological periods they're from.

primate A biological order that contains species related to
monkeys, apes, and humans.

primatology The study of nonhuman primates.

FURTHER READING

BOOKS

Bright, Michael. *The Evolution of You and Me*. New York, NY: PowerKids Press, 2018.

Heitkamp, Kristina Lyn. *The Rift Valley and the Archaeological Evidence of the First Humans*. New York, NY: Rosen Publishing, 2017.

Huddle, Rusty. *Human Evolution*. New York, NY: Rosen Publishing/Britannica Educational Publishing, 2017.

Jobes, Cecily. *Fossils*. New York, NY: PowerKids Press, 2017.

Sol90 Editorial Staff. *A Visual Guide to Evolution and Genetics*. New York, NY: Rosen Young Adult, 2019.

WEBSITES

Leakey: A Century of the Family in East Africa
Leakey.com
Learn more about the Leakeys' discoveries, follow ongoing work in the Turkana Basin based on the Leakeys' work, and find family member biographies.

The Leakey Foundation
leakeyfoundation.org
Read even more about the Leakey family, their important research accomplishments, and how their legacy lives on through this foundation's work.

Turkana Basin Institute
turkanabasin.org
Created by Richard Leakey in conjunction with Stony Brook University, this institute ensures year-round research continues in eastern Africa and provides the public with interesting information about the paleoanthropological research being done.

WildLife Direct
wildlifedirect.org
Richard Leakey's conservation organization highlights the many perils Africa's endangered animals face and partners with governments and educational programs to carry out campaigns to save Africa's wildlife.

INDEX